D1063798

CAREERS IN THE
BUILDING TRADES

A GROWING DEMAND

Flooring Installer

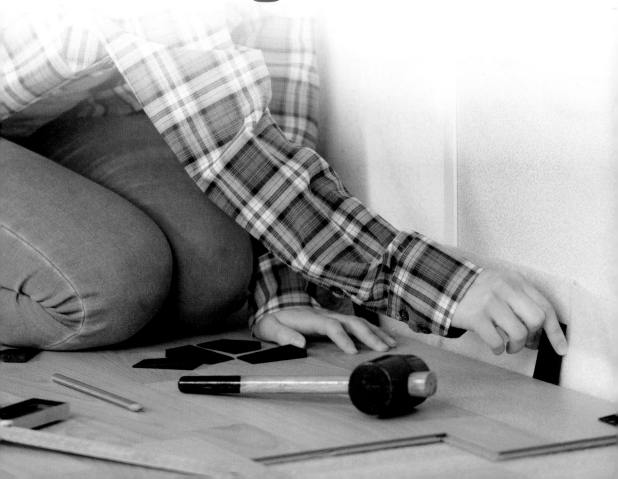

Careers in the Building Trades

A Growing Demand

 Apprenticeships

 Carpenter

 Construction & Building Inspector

 Electrician

 Flooring Installer

 Heating and Cooling Technician

 Masonry Worker

 Plumber

 Roofer

Working in Green Construction

CAREERS IN THE
BUILDING TRADES

A GROWING DEMAND

Flooring Installer

Andrew Morkes

MASON CREST

Mason Crest
450 Parkway Drive, Suite D
Broomall, Pennsylvania 19008
(866) MCP-BOOK (toll-free)
www.masoncrest.com

First printing

9 8 7 6 5 4 3 2 1
ISBN (hardback) 978-1-4222-4115-8

ISBN (series) 978-1-4222-4110-3

ISBN (ebook) 978-1-4222-7685-3

Cataloging-in-Publication Data on file with the Library of Congress

NATIONAL
HIGHLIGHTS

Developed and Produced by National Highlights Inc.
Proofreader: Mika Jin
Interior and cover design: Yolanda Van Cooten
Production: Michelle Luke

CONTENTS

KEY ICONS TO LOOK FOR:

 Words to understand: These words with their easy-to-understand definitions will increase the reader's understanding of the text while building vocabulary skills.

 Sidebars: This boxed material within the main text allows readers to build knowledge, gain insights, explore possibilities, and broaden their perspectives by weaving together additional information to provide realistic and holistic perspectives.

 Educational Videos: Readers can view videos by scanning our QR codes, providing them with additional educational content to supplement the text. Examples include news coverage, moments in history, speeches, iconic sports moments and much more!

 Text-dependent questions: These questions send the reader back to the text for more careful attention to the evidence presented there.

 Research projects: Readers are pointed toward areas of further inquiry connected to each chapter. Suggestions are provided for projects that encourage deeper research and analysis.

 Series glossary of key terms: This back-of-the-book glossary contains terminology used throughout this series. Words found here increase the reader's ability to read and comprehend higher-level books and articles in this field.

INTRODUCTION

The Trades: Great Careers, Good Money, and Other Rewards

Trades workers play a major role in the success of economies throughout the world. They keep the power on (electricians); install and repair pipes that carry water, fuel, and other liquids to, from, and within businesses, factories, and homes (plumbers and pipefitters); and lay and finish tile, wood, vinyl, carpet, and other types of flooring (flooring installers); among many other job duties. Yet despite their pivotal role in our society, only 6 percent of students consider a career in the trades, according to ExploretheTrades.org. Why? Because many young people have misconceptions about the trades. They have been told that the trades are low-paying, lack job security, and other untruths. In fact, working in the trades is one of the best career choices you can make. The following paragraphs provide more information on why a career in the trades is a good idea.

Good pay. Contrary to public perception, skilled trades workers earn salaries that place them firmly in the middle class. Average yearly salaries for construction workers in the United States are $48,900, according to the U.S. Department of Labor. This salary is slightly higher than the average earnings for some careers that require a bachelor's or graduate degree—including recreational therapists, $48,190; child, family, and school social workers, $47,510; and mental health counselors, $46,050. Trades workers who become managers or who launch their own businesses can have earnings that range from $90,000 to $200,000.

Strong employment prospects. There are shortages of trades workers throughout the world, according to the human resource consulting firm ManpowerGroup. In fact, trades workers are the most in-demand occupational field in the Americas, Europe,

the Middle East, and Africa. They ranked fourth in the Asia-Pacific region. Tile workers are in especially strong demand in Canada, Sweden, Russia, and Australia, according to the recruitment firm Michael Page. Employment for flooring installers in the United States is expected to grow faster than the average for all careers during the next decade.

Provides a comfortable life without a bachelor's or graduate degree. For decades in the United States and other countries, there has been an emphasis on earning a college degree as the key to life success. But studies show that only 35 percent of future jobs in the United States will require a four-year degree or higher. With college tuition continuing to increase and the chances of landing a good job out of college decreasing, a growing number of people are entering apprenticeship programs to prepare for careers in the trades. And unlike college students, apprentices receive a salary while learning and they don't have to pay off loans after they complete their education. It's a good feeling to start your career without $50,000 to $200,000 in college loans.

Rewarding work environment and many career options. A career in the trades is fulfilling because you get to use both your hands and your head to solve problems and make the world a better place. Flooring installers and repairers work at homes, commercial building construction sites, in historical restoration, or in other places where floors need to be built or repaired. Many trades workers launch their own businesses.

Jobs can't be offshored. Trades careers involve hands-on work that requires the worker to be on-site to do his or her job. As a result, there is no chance that your position will be offshored to a foreign country. In an uncertain employment atmosphere, that's encouraging news.

Job opportunities are available throughout the United States and the world. There is a need for trades workers in small towns and big cities. If demand for their skills is not strong in their geographic area, they can move to other cities, states, or countries where demand is higher.

Are the Trades Right for Me?

Test your interest in the trades. How many of these statements do you agree with?

☐ **My favorite class in school is shop.**

☐ **I like to build and repair things.**

☐ **I like doing household repairs.**

☐ **I like to use power and hand tools.**

☐ **I like projects that allow me to work with my hands and use my creativity.**

☐ **I enjoy observing work at construction sites.**

☐ **I like to watch home-repair shows on TV and the internet.**

☐ **I don't mind getting dirty when I work on a project.**

☐ **I am good at math.**

If many of the statements above describe you, then you should consider a career in the trades. But you don't need to select a career right now. Check out this book on a career as a flooring installer and other books in the series to learn more about occupational paths in the trades. Good luck with your career exploration!

■ *There are good opportunities for women in the flooring industry.*

Words to Understand

building codes: Rules established by local, state, regional, and national governments that ensure safe construction.

mudroom: A room that is located next to or near the front or back door of a home in which footwear and coats can be removed and stored before a person enters the rest of the home. Mudrooms sometimes contain sinks and washers and dryers.

textile: Flexible material that is made up of natural or synthetic (human-made) fibers. Textiles include clothing, wall coverings, and floor coverings (such as carpeting).

veneer: In wood floor installation, a thin slice of wood—usually thinner than one-eighth of an inch (three millimeters) that is glued atop the other panels.

CHAPTER 1

What Do Flooring Installers Do?

Without flooring, a house would just be four walls. There would be nothing to walk on and, to be a little silly, nowhere to put our couches, chairs, desks, and bookshelves. All kidding aside, floors are a key part of any building, and floor installers build and repair floors of all types. These include those made of hardwood, wood laminate, carpeting, stone, cork, vinyl, and other materials. Some flooring installers specialize in installing a certain type of flooring (such as carpeting), while others install many types of flooring. Flooring installers work for construction companies, small contractors, and government agencies. Others operate their own businesses.

There are many ways to prepare to become a flooring installer. Some people train by participating in an apprenticeship program. Others earn certificates or associate degrees in construction technology, which include classes in flooring installation, carpentry, and masonry. Still others learn through informal methods such as working as a helper to an experienced flooring installer and taking classes offered by colleges and professional associations to build their skills. Many cities, states, and countries require flooring contractors to be licensed. Some installers become certified to show customers that they have met the highest standards established by their industry.

This is a great career for those who enjoy working with their hands, who like to use their problem-solving and critical-thinking skills as they install new floors and repair existing ones, and who want the opportunity to make a good living without earning a four-year degree.

■ *A carpet installer cuts carpeting.*

Hardwood floors are becoming an in-demand feature for home buyers, according to the National Association of Realtors. It reports that 25 percent of buyers under the age of thirty-five, and 28 percent of those between age thirty-five and fifty-four, viewed hardwood floors as "very important" when looking for a home. Only 17 percent of those ages fifty-five and older felt the same way.

■ *Learn about the work of carpet installers:*

Types of Flooring Installers

The job duties of flooring installers vary depending on their employer, what types of flooring they install or repair, and other factors. But most perform the following duties:

- Measure flooring areas to calculate the quantities of materials that will be needed

- Provide estimates to customers that detail the cost to install or repair a floor

- Remove existing flooring and clean (scrape off old adhesives or other components) and level the surface that will be covered

- In some instances, install a subfloor which the tile, wood, or other material will be placed on (sometimes the subfloor is installed by carpenters or other construction trades workers)

- Cut or otherwise prepare carpeting, tile, or other building materials for installation
- Mix mastic or prepare adhesives (tile, carpeting, and other types of flooring) or, if installing hardwood floors, prepare the nail gun, adhesives, or other joining materials
- Arrange flooring according to the design
- Install flooring using nails, staples, or adhesives
- Fill flooring joints with filler compound and clean up any excess compound (tile installation)
- Use a cutting tool to trim excess carpet or linoleum
- Apply necessary finishes, such as stains and sealants
- Follow applicable **building codes** during the entire process

Some flooring installers also install stone and tile on countertops, walls, and other non-floor surfaces.

Here are some of the most popular career paths in flooring installation.

Carpet Installers

Carpet is a **textile** floor covering that used to be made of wool, but which is now more often made of synthetic (human-made) fibers such as nylon, polypropylene, or polyester. Carpeting is an extremely popular floor covering because it is more comfortable, warmer, and less expensive than many other types of flooring. It is typically installed in living rooms, family rooms, bedrooms, and hallways, but not usually in bathrooms and kitchens. *Carpet installers* use a variety of tools such as carpet knives (to cut carpet segments), knee kickers (to position the carpet), power stretchers (to pull the carpet snugly against walls), carpet seam irons (to join the seams on two pieces of carpet), and hammers (to nail down tack strips around the perimeter of the room) to do their jobs.

A related profession is *carpet tile installer*. These workers glue small, modular pieces of carpet to the subfloor. Some people prefer carpet tiles to traditional carpeting because these tiles can be arranged to create attractive and interesting designs and because they are easy to replace if torn, stained, or otherwise damaged.

Wood Flooring Installers

Hardwood floors are extremely popular choices for installation in homes and other buildings. There are many species of hardwood that are used in flooring, including oak, maple, walnut, Douglas fir, cherry, cypress, and ash. Customers like hardwood because it is attractive and durable. Hardwood comes in many colors. For example, white ash is light in color, while walnut is darker.

There are several types of wood flooring. Hardwood flooring consists of a solid piece of wood. Engineered wood is real wood, but it is made out of multiple pieces of wood (from the same or different species) or wood composite **veneers**. Laminate flooring is another type of wood flooring material (although it is constructed of wood fibers, and it is not wood in the sense of being in its natural state like solid wood flooring or engineered wood). It is made out of sheets of synthetic pressed wood. It has a top layer that is created to mimic the look of hardwood or stone flooring. Hardwood, engineered, and laminate floors are installed throughout homes and other structures.

Some installers lay softwood (pine, fir, cypress, cedar, spruce, hemlock, etc.) floors. This type of wood is less expensive than hardwood flooring, but more susceptible to dents and dings. Softwood floors are also more environmentally friendly than slower-growing

■ *A close-up of damage caused by the powderpost beetle.*

Wood Bug Pests

Insects can sometimes damage wood flooring. For example, termites, insects that feed on dead plants and wood, can chew on wood floors. They are more apt to feed on softwood floors (pine, fir, etc.) rather than hardwood floors. Signs of termite damage include squeaky floors or a hollow sound when walking. Minor damage can be fixed with wood filler, but significant damage requires the replacement of entire wood boards. Termites can also damage the underlying floor of laminate. In this instance, the flooring must be replaced. Termites can cause serious damage to homes. In fact, termites cost Americans more than $5 billion in damage each year, according to Orkin.

Another pest is the lyctid beetle, which is also known as the powderpost beetle. These beetles may already be present in other wood components (wood furniture, cabinets, etc.) or their eggs may already be laid in the pores of the wood that arrives for installation. The larvae hatch, feed on the wood, and eventually leave the wood, creating small pinholes. They are most likely to be found in hardwood floors. These beetles can be eliminated by applying insecticides (chemicals) or by removing the affected areas of wood.

Sources: Orkin, National Wood Flooring Association

hardwoods. People often install softwood floors in rooms that don't get a heavy amount of foot traffic.

Wood flooring installers lay wood flooring components and join them using adhesives, nails, screws, or other materials. In some types of floors—known as floating floors—the boards are not attached to the subfloor by an adhesive or screws, nails, or staples. Instead, the installer connects the boards to one another (either by a click-fitting or tongue-and-groove process, or by an adhesive). If an unfinished hardwood floor is installed, the installer uses a floor sander to finish the job by sanding the wood, then applies stains (to color the wood) and sealants (to protect the wood from water and everyday wear and tear). At some job sites, *floor sanders and finishers* handle these duties.

■ *An installer lays ceramic tile.*

Tile Installers

Tile flooring is made out of ceramics (such as porcelain), marble, wood, or other types of building materials. It is a popular flooring material in kitchens, bathrooms, mudrooms, enclosed porches or sunrooms, and lobbies of hotels and office buildings, but it can also be installed in other rooms and settings.

Tile installers lay and set tiles on floors, walls, and ceilings by taking the following steps:

- Measuring the area to be covered and calculating how much tile will be needed
- Cleaning the area where the tiles will be placed
- Preparing and applying cement, glue, or other adhesives
- Cutting and fitting tiles
- Tamping them down as they work to remove air bubbles and assure a tight fit
- Using squares and levels to align tiles as they are installed, and straightening as necessary
- Inserting spacers between the tiles so that the tile stays the same distance from one another until the adhesives dry
- Applying plaster between tiles and removing excess plaster
- Once the adhesive is dry, wiping the tiles for a clean, attractive look

Terrazzo Masons

Terrazzo is made of chips of marble, glass, or other aggregates (a combination of several elements) that are placed in colored cement, then ground smooth and polished to a beautiful shine. *Terrazzo masons*, who are also known as *terrazzo workers* and *finishers*, create decorative terrazzo floors, patios, and other structures. Much of their set-up work (pouring, leveling, and finishing concrete) is similar to what cement masons do. Once the concrete or other building material (epoxy, resin) has been poured or applied, terrazzo workers create decorative finishes by creatively placing fine marble chips into concrete or other material. Once the terrazzo sets, masons fix any depressions or imperfections with a grinder or hand tools to create a smooth and attractive finish.

■ *Watch a beautiful terrazzo floor being installed:*

Resilient Flooring Installers

Resilient flooring is made from synthetic materials that are elastic. This type of flooring is popular because it is durable, inexpensive, resistant to water damage, and less noisy than other types of flooring. Types of residential resilient flooring include residential sheet vinyl, luxury vinyl tile, vinyl tile, and linoleum. In homes, resilient flooring is often installed in kitchens, mudrooms, bathrooms, laundry rooms, and basements. In commercial settings, types of resilient materials include commercial sheet vinyl linoleum, vinyl composition tile, bio-based tile, rubber sheet, and rubber tile.

Resilient floor layers cut flooring into the desired size and use glue to put it into place. They often use a floor roller to smooth, flatten, and ultimately bond the resilient flooring material to the adhesive.

Work Environments

The majority of flooring work is done indoors, so you'll work in climate-controlled settings for the most part. Flooring is typically installed after most of the other construction tasks have been finished on a project, so work sites are typically clean, or at least not cluttered with building materials. Tile installers and terrazzo masons work outdoors, but not in the rain.

■ *Installers wear hearing protection and masks to stay safe on the job.*

Most flooring installers work forty hours a week, Monday through Friday—although longer hours (including weekends) may be necessary when a project is on deadline. For commercial projects, flooring installers work at night and on weekends so as not to disturb regular business operations.

Although the career of flooring installer is not as dangerous as that of roofer, mason, or electrician, injuries and accidents can occur on the job. To protect themselves, flooring installers wear safety glasses, knee pads, heavy gloves, earplugs (when using saws), dust masks or respirators (to protect themselves from breathing in dust or other toxic substances such as silica, as well as fumes from solvents), and protective clothing to prevent injury.

Related Careers

Flooring installers who complete specialized education and training are qualified to work in many related fields. Here are a few popular options:

Masonry workers, who are sometimes known as masons, use brick, tile, cement, stone (marble, granite, limestone, etc.), and other materials to create surfaces and structures such as buildings, walls, fences, fireplaces, bridges, roads, sidewalks, and other structures. Many aspiring masons prepare for the field by completing an apprenticeship. Others participate in training programs at technical schools or learn via on-the-job training.

Construction inspectors examine buildings and other structures to ensure that they have been built correctly. *Building inspectors* examine homes, condominiums, townhomes, and other new or previously owned buildings. They are also known as *home inspectors*. Some inspectors specialize in examining the condition of structural masonry. Many inspectors have earned a certificate or an associate degree that includes courses in building inspection, construction technology, and home inspection. Some also receive certification from the Masonry Institute of America.

Framing carpenters measure, cut, and assemble wood and other materials to create the basic framework for floor, wall, and roof framing, window installation, and exterior door installation. They are also known as *rough carpenters*. Carpenters train for the field by completing an apprenticeship or on-the-job training, earning a certificate or associate degree from a community or technical college, or receiving training in the military.

The Pros and Cons of Starting Your Own Floor Installation Business

 About 36 percent of carpet, floor, and tile installers and finishers in the United States are self-employed, according to the U.S. Department of Labor. Self-employed workers are those who own a business, rather than work for a corporation or other employer. Here are some of the pros and cons of being a flooring contractor:

Pros

- You get to be your own boss.
- You can create your own work schedule (e.g., work extra one day, so you can take the next day off to go hiking or extend your weekend).
- You can make more money than a salaried flooring installer if your business is successful.

Cons

- It can be stressful to keep your business running smoothly.
- You don't get a regular salary; you have to get customers in order to make money. If there's no work, there's no money.
- You'll be responsible for advertising your business, preparing estimates, scheduling appointments, and managing staff.
- Contractors typically work much longer hours—especially when launching their businesses—than salaried flooring installers do.

Cost estimators are experts in one or more construction specialties (masonry, floor installation, electrical, etc.). They create estimates of how much money, time, materials, and labor will be required to complete a construction project or create a product. Cost estimators who work in the construction industry typically need a bachelor's degree in construction management, engineering, or a related field.

Plasterers apply plaster to ceilings, interior walls, and other areas of buildings, as well as to wire, wood, or metal. Plasterers prepare for the field via an apprenticeship or on-the-job training.

Construction managers oversee every aspect of a construction project—from the various types of trades workers (electricians, plumbers, steelworkers, etc. that do the actual work), to managing budgets, to ordering supplies and equipment, to ensuring that the job site is safe for workers. They typically have a lot of experience in the construction industry and a bachelor's degree in construction management.

■ *Some flooring installers pursue additional education to become construction managers.*

Text-Dependent Questions

1. What is carpeting made from?

2. What are the pros and cons of owning a flooring business?

3. What are some careers that are related to that of flooring installer?

Research Project

Talk to a flooring installer about what it's like to own a business. Ask if you can job shadow him or her in the office and at job sites.

CHAPTER 2

Tools of the Trade

Cutting, Pounding, Application, Joining, and Finishing Tools

carpet seam iron: A tool that is used to join the seams on two pieces of carpet.

carpet stretcher: A tool that is comprised of expandable poles, a fulcrum arm, and a head that has teeth on it that is used to grab and stretch carpeting. The back-end of the carpet stretcher is placed at the wall where the carpet stretching will begin, and leverage is used to stretch the carpeting as the carpet installer presses the fulcrum arm as he or she moves toward the opposite wall. Also called a **power stretcher**.

chisel: A hand tool with a shaped, sharp cutting edge that is used to cut, chip, or carve stone, wood, or metal.

finish applicator: A hand tool that is equipped with a long handle and a roller that is used to apply finishing sealant to hardwood floors.

floor roller: A hand tool that has two hand grips, a long pole, and a base roller or series of rollers that is used to smooth, flatten, and ultimately bond vinyl, carpet, linoleum, and other floor coverings to adhesive that has been previously applied to the floor below the coverings.

floor scraper: A handheld tool that is used to scrape old adhesives, paint overspray, drywall mud, and other lightweight contaminants from the subfloor in preparation for laying a new floor.

flooring nailer: A pneumatic (air powered) or manual device that is used to nail hardwood panels to the subfloor. May also be known as a **flooring cleat nailer**.

flooring stapler: A pneumatic or manual device that anchors the flooring planks to the subfloor; it drives staples into the wood planking.

hammer: A hand tool with a metal or wooden head that is mounted to the handle at right angles. Flooring installers use hammers to tap wood flooring into place, to drive or remove nails, to break-up old construction materials, or to perform other tasks during the building process.

hand saw: A cutting tool with a long, thin, serrated steel blade; it is operated using a backward and forward movement.

knee kicker: A tool that is used to position the carpet and smooth out any wrinkles in the carpeting.

power saw: A saw that is used to cut large quantities of wood, stone, or other building materials. It is available in both a hand-held or table-mounted model.

sander: A power tool that uses sandpaper or other abrasive material to smooth a surface.

tapered-edged foam brush: A handheld brush that is used to apply adhesives or cleaners in between tiles.

tile scribe: A sharp hand tool that is used to cut tile. May also be known as a **tile cutter**.

trowel: A flat-bladed hand tool with a V-shaped or square plate that is used to pick up and spread mortar.

utility knife: A tool—often with a retractable blade—that is used to cut vinyl and other material.

wet saw: A saw that is equipped with a water hose that sprays water on the blade as the cut is made to reduce the creation of high levels of crystalline silica (tiny specks of concrete, sandstone, granite, and brick that can cause serious health problems if inhaled). The use of a wet saw also helps equipment to last longer.

Measuring and Investigative Tools

chalk line: A marking tool that is used by tradesworkers to snap chalk lines to get the alignment correct for flooring, walls, or other structures or components during construction.

framing square: A measuring device that has a long arm and a shorter arm, which intersect at a right angle (90 degrees). It is used as a guide when flooring installers, carpenters, and other tradesworkers draw lines on materials before cutting, or for locating holes. Also known as a **carpenter's square**.

laser measure: A device that allows users to take distance measurements instantly.

level: A device that is used to establish a horizontal plane. It is comprised of a small glass tube that contains alcohol or a similar liquid and an air bubble.

moisture meter: A handheld device that can either find elevated moisture levels hidden behind tile, vinyl, wood, or other building materials beneath shower and bathroom floors, or actually measure the elevated moisture levels by touching the material with two pins on the device. Some meters can perform both functions.

tape measure: A flexible ruler made of fiber glass, a metal strip, cloth, or plastic.

Safety and Access Gear and Equipment

dust mask: A protective covering worn over the mouth and nose to reduce the inhalation of dust and other airborne pollutants.

knee pads: Protective padding that is worn around the knees to protect the wearer from strain and pain on the jobsite.

respirator: An artificial breathing device that protects the wearer from breathing dust, smoke, crystalline silica (tiny specks of concrete, sandstone, granite, and brick that can cause serious health problems if inhaled), or other toxic substances.

safety glasses: Protective gear that shields the eyes from injury by stone or wood chips, protruding nails, and other objects.

Computer and Recording Technology

building information modeling software: A computer application that uses a 3D model-based process that helps construction, architecture, and engineering professionals to more efficiently plan, design, build, and manage buildings and infrastructure.

hygrometer: A digital tool that is used to check the relative humidity at a job site. Wood flooring that is installed in an environment with too-high humidity may experience cupping or other problems.

office and customer management software: Computer applications that help users track finances and manage billing, schedule appointments, draft correspondence, and perform other tasks.

CHAPTER 3
Terms of the Trade

adhesive: A substance such as glue or contact cement that can be used to bond material together by surface attachment.

baseboard: A thin piece of wood that covers the lowest part of an interior wall. It is used to cover the joint between the floor and the wall. Also known as **floor molding**, **base molding**, and **skirting board**.

bleeding: A negative development in which stone is stained by corrosive metals, oil-based putties, caulking, sealing compounds, minerals in the stone, or other compounds.

blueprints: A reproduction of a technical plan for the construction of a home or other structure. Blueprints are created by licensed architects.

brick: A solid or partly hollow rectangular block of clay that has been baked in a kiln (oven) or by the sun until it is hard. Bricks are frequently used to construct walls and other structures, as well as for paving material.

buckling: The unwanted bending of a building material—such as flooring or a door frame—as a result of wear and tear, the pressure of heavy weight, or contact with a substance such as water.

building codes: A series of rules established by local, state, regional, and national governments that ensure safe construction.

carpet: A textile floor covering that used to be made of wool, but is now more often made of synthetic fibers such as nylon, polypropylene, or polyester.

caulk: Waterproof filler and sealant that is used to fill spaces around windows and doors, shower stalls and bathtubs, and joints that may exist between floors and fixtures. Deteriorating caulking can allow the intrusion of water and cause damage to floors, walls, and other building components.

cement: The binding element in both mortar and concrete, which is most frequently made of limestone, clay, silica sand, shells, and other materials. The most commonly-used type of cement is Portland cement. It is manufactured from limestone and clay. It is further categorized as a hydraulic cement because it hardens when combined with water.

click-fitting system: A wood flooring system in which the flooring planks click into place and lock together so that there is no need for glue, nails, or screws.

concrete: A common construction material that is made of sand, conglomerate gravel, pebbles, broken stone, or slag (stony waste) in a mortar or cement matrix.

cupping: Occurs when moisture content levels are different between the bottom of the flooring and its top portion (as a result of improper construction, a broken water pipe, and other factors). When this unwanted reaction happens, the sides of each flooring board are higher than the center of the board.

delamination: The most serious issue that can happen to wall-to-wall carpeting, in which the carpet's secondary backing is separated from its primary backing. When carpeting becomes delaminated, it becomes wrinkled and cannot be restretched.

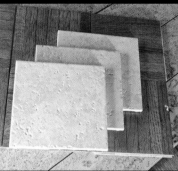

floating wood floor: A type of floor that is installed over wood or concrete subfloors, but in which the boards are not attached to the subfloor by an adhesive or screws, nails, or staples. Floating floor boards are connected to one another (either by a click-fitting or tongue-and-groove process, or by an adhesive). Floating wood floors are often very stable and strong, and they are less prone to expansion and contraction.

flooring tile: Flooring that is made out of ceramics, marble, wood, or other types of building materials.

green construction: The planning, design, construction, and operation of structures in an environmentally responsible manner. Green construction stresses energy and water efficiency, the use of eco-friendly construction materials (when possible), indoor environmental quality, and the structure's overall effects on its site or the larger community. Also known as green building.

groundwater: Water from a subsurface water source. If a building's basement is not properly insulated, groundwater can get into the basement and cause damage to flooring and walls and create mold.

grout: A mixture of Portland cement and sand that is used to fill the seams between masonry units such as tiles.

joint: The space between masonry units or a wall and the floor.

joists: A series of parallel, horizontal components of wood, engineered wood, or steel that support a ceiling or floor. Joists are supported by beams, wall framing, and foundations.

laminate flooring: Flooring material that is made out of sheets of synthetic pressed wood; it has a top layer that is created to mimic the look of hardwood or stone flooring.

masonry: Construction using durable materials such as tile, brick, cement, stone (marble, granite, limestone, etc.), or similar materials.

masonry units: An individual brick or block in masonry construction.

mortar: A mixture of cement, sand, lime, and water that is used to link masonry units.

subfloor: The bottom-most layer of a floor that rests on the joists. The underlayment and then the top floor (carpet, tile, etc.) are installed atop the subfloor.

tack strip: A strip of wood that has very sharp tacks protruding through it at 60-degree angles. Tack strips run the entire perimeter of a room and hold wall-to-wall carpeting in place and keep carpeting stretched out.

tongue-and-groove system: A common method of joining two pieces of wood flooring in which each piece of wood has a protruding tongue side and a receiving groove side.

transition: A thin piece of wood or metal that affixes to the floor area in the doorway between rooms.

terrazzo: A type of flooring that consists of chips of marble, glass, or other aggregates (a combination of several elements) that are placed in colored cement, then ground smooth and polished to a beautiful shine.

tile spacers: Small pieces of plastic (most commonly) that are used to space tiles an equal distance from one another.

underlayment: A layer of felt that is placed between the underfloor and hardwood or laminate flooring to provide water protection, sound proofing, and cushioning.

vinyl flooring: Flooring material that is made out of plastic, and which is highly-resistant to water damage.

wet-cutting: A process in which stone is cut with a saw that is equipped with a water hose that sprays water on the blade as the cut is made to reduce the creation of high levels of crystalline silica (tiny specks of concrete, sandstone, granite, and brick that can cause serious health problems if inhaled). Wet-cutting also helps equipment to last longer since the water reduces the amount of heat and dust generated by the cutting process—therefore reducing wear and tear.

wood spacers: Wedges or blocks (some models are adjustable) that allow the flooring installer to leave a small space around the perimeter of the room so that the wood flooring can expand and contract based on levels of humidity.

■ Taking chemistry classes will provide a good introduction to the chemical properties of various materials and help you to develop your problem-solving skills.

Words to Understand

continuing education: A form of education that is completed after one finishes his or her primary training (college, apprenticeship, etc.) for a job. Workers take continuing education classes and webinars throughout their careers to improve their skills, to learn about new types of technology or building methods, or to prepare to become certified.

fringe benefits: A payment or non-financial benefit that is given to a worker in addition to salary. These consist of cash bonuses for good work, paid vacations and sick days, and health and life insurance.

Registered Apprenticeship program: One that meets standards of fairness, safety, and training established by the U.S. government or local governments.

webinar: A class that is offered on the internet.

work estimate: A written summary prepared by a contractor that details the work that will need to be done (e.g., new tile installed, terrazzo floor repaired, etc.) and the estimated cost of the work and building materials.

CHAPTER 4

Preparing for the Field and Making a Living

Educational Paths

There's no single way to train to become a flooring installer. Some train by participating in an apprenticeship program. Others earn certificates or associate degrees in construction technology, which include classes in carpentry, masonry, and flooring installation from community colleges or technical colleges. Still others learn through informal methods such as working as a helper to an experienced flooring installer and taking classes and webinars offered by colleges and professional associations to build their skills. You can be successful as a flooring installer by training in any of these ways.

High School Classes

Before you head to college, start an apprenticeship, or get hired as a helper, you should use your high school years to take some classes that will give you good general preparation for a career in the construction industry. Take the following classes:

■ *An apprentice (left) learns how to install flooring.*

- **Shop** classes will teach you about the use of hand and power tools; construction techniques; safety practices; and building, troubleshooting, and fixing things.

- **Mathematics** courses (especially algebra and geometry) will give you the skills to determine the amount of flooring material you'll need to cover a particular space; how to mix the right amounts of grout or mortar; evaluate numerical information on blueprints, building plans, and diagrams; and, if you own a flooring business, create **work estimates**, prepare invoices, manage budgets, and set payroll. Business, accounting, computer science, marketing, and English/writing classes will also come in handy if you decide to become a flooring contractor.

- **Chemistry** classes will provide a good introduction to the chemical properties of various materials. You'll also learn how to identify and solve problems that occur during lab experiments. These troubleshooting and critical-thinking skills will come in handy on the job.

- **Art** courses will help you to develop the creative ability and artistic skills you'll need if you install terrazzo or other decorative flooring.

- **Foreign language** classes will be useful because, in many countries, people speak a variety of languages. Knowing a foreign language will come in handy if you work with people or have customers who do not speak your language. For example, English is the dominant language in the United States, but Spanish is spoken in many areas where many immigrants or people of Latino heritage live. In some cities, Mandarin, Polish, or other languages may be commonly spoken.

Pre-Apprenticeships

Some people who are interested in becoming flooring installers participate in pre-apprenticeship programs before entering an apprenticeship program. The U.S. Department of Labor says that there are many benefits to participating in a pre-apprenticeship program, including:

- Allows you to investigate and learn about career options

- Allows you to receive classroom- and technology-based training

- Builds your math, English, literacy, and work-readiness skills that employers want in apprentices and employees

- Prepares you to advance into a **Registered Apprenticeship program**.

Pre-apprenticeship programs are offered by unions, professional associations, and community colleges. In the United States, pre-apprenticeship programs last anywhere from six to twelve weeks, although longer programs may be part of an apprenticeship. For example, INSTALL—Installation Standards Training Alliance, an organization that is associated with the floor covering arm of the United Brotherhood of Carpenters and Joiners, offers a one-year pre-apprenticeship program as part of its five-year flooring apprenticeship program.

The International Masonry Training and Education Foundation provides pre-apprenticeship training in the trowel trades: brick, stone, tile, marble, terrazzo, refractory, plaster, cement, and pointing/cleaning/caulking.

In the United States, Associated Builders and Contractors offers a pre-apprenticeship program that prepares students to enter a registered apprenticeship program. Some of the modules completed by participants include:

- Introduction to Construction Math
- Introduction to Hand Tools
- Introduction to Power Tools
- Introduction to Construction Drawings
- Introduction to Material Handling

The National Association of Home Builders offers pre-apprenticeship certificate training through the Home Builders Institute. The program is geared toward high school and college students, transitioning military members, veterans, justice-involved youth and adults, and unemployed and displaced workers. Programs are available in masonry (including flooring), plumbing, carpentry, building construction technology, weatherization, electrical, landscaping, and painting. In the masonry program, participants learn how to mix mortar and grout, lay brick floors and stairs, and use green building techniques.

Apprenticeships

Participating in an apprenticeship is a popular way to become a flooring installer. In the United States, flooring apprenticeships typically last two to five years. During each year in the program, trainees complete 2,000 hours of on-the-job training and 144 hours of related classroom instruction. Apprentices are paid a salary that increases as they obtain experience. Entry requirements vary by program, but typical requirements include:

■ *Many flooring installers receive their training by working as helpers to experienced professionals.*

- Minimum age of eighteen (in Canada and some other countries, the minimum age is sixteen)
- High school education
- One year of high school algebra
- Qualifying score on an aptitude test
- Drug free (illegal drugs)

INSTALL—Installation Standards Training Alliance offers a five-year flooring apprenticeship program. Its curriculum has nine components. Here are the components and some of the topics covered in each:

- **Standard Skills:** hand and power tools, flooring and adhesive removal equipment and methods, adhesives and fundamentals of adhesives application, general and complex layout and installation

- **Safety:** hazard communication and chemical safety, first aid, how to safely use power tools, working in confined spaces

- **Productivity:** employability skills, diverse working environments, staging of materials, installation procedures

- **Green Building Awareness:** the benefits of green building, working in accordance with green building standards, how to create less material waste, recycling

- **Carpet:** carpet construction, tools, layouts, hand sewing, carpet tile, tackstrip and cushion installation, stretch-in carpet installation

- **Resilient Flooring:** tools, products, layout, sheet layout, seam cutting, repairs

- **Resinous Flooring:** types and characteristics of products, tools and testing equipment, mixing and installation of resins

- **Hardwood Flooring:** equipment operation and maintenance; types of fillers, stains and finishes; recoating and refinishing existing floors; board replacement and blending finishes

- **Concrete Polishing:** understanding the chemistry of concrete, wet vs. dry polishing, surface preparation and existing coating removal, grit selection, stains, dyes, and stencils.

The International Union of Painters and Allied Trades' Finishing Trades Institute also offers an apprenticeship program for flooring installers. It partners with Mountwest Community and Technical College in Huntington, West Virginia, in the United States. Apprentices can earn up to forty college credits by completing the apprenticeship.

Visit http://www.doleta.gov/OA/sainformation.cfm for information on apprenticeship training programs in the United States. If you live in another country, contact your nation's department of labor to learn more about training programs. Those who complete an apprenticeship are known as journeymen flooring installers.

Technical and Community College

It will be hard to find a technical or community college that offers a certificate or associate degree in flooring installation. But some aspiring flooring installers head to college to earn certificates or degrees in general construction and take classes in floor installation. Since flooring installers perform some of the same tasks as masonry workers, it is a good idea to take classes or earn a certificate in masonry.

On-the-Job Training

Some flooring installers learn their skills by first working as helpers to experienced installers. In the beginning, you'll do basic tasks such as moving and setting up supplies and equipment, removing old tile, and cleaning floor surfaces. Gradually, you'll be given more challenging tasks, such as mixing mortar, cutting tile or carpet, and installing floor coverings. On-the-job training, which is usually combined with flooring installation classes offered by a college or association, typically lasts two to three years. At the end of this time, you'll be considered a full-fledged installer. You'll be offered a job or, if there are no jobs available, you can start your own company or work for another firm.

■ *Building relationships with your coworkers is a good way to network.*

Community vs. Technical College

A community college is a private or public two-year school that awards certificates and associate degrees, and sometimes bachelor's degrees. A technical college is a public or private college that offers two- or four-year programs in practical subjects, such as the trades, information technology, applied sciences, agriculture, and engineering.

Getting a Job

After you complete your training, you'll need to get a job. While you're not in the job market now, it's a good idea to learn the different ways people get jobs so that you're ready to start your search once you finish your training. You might get a job offer through your apprenticeship program or through your college's career services office, but if not, try these popular job-search strategies:

■ *Learn some networking do's and don'ts:*

Start Networking. Networking is one of the most important job-search tools. In fact, 80 percent of workers surveyed by LinkedIn believe that professional networking is important to career success. Networking might seem scary, but it really just involves talking to people you know and reaching out to people you don't know to see if they

The Pros and Cons of Installer Training Paths

Apprenticeship

Pros: Provides a direct path to employment. You'll make money while you learn (unlike college), and your salary increases as you gain experience. College credit is available for some coursework. Employers respect applicants who completed an apprenticeship.

Con: Programs last two to five years.

A Good Fit: For those who like a structured environment that combines both classroom and hands-on training.

Technical School/Community College

Pros: Programs are shorter than most apprenticeships—typically one to two years.

Cons: You must pay tuition and you do not get paid like apprentices do.

A Good Fit: For those who want to enter the workforce more quickly.

On-the-Job Training

Pros: Allows you to get to work right away and receive a salary.

Cons: Training might not be as detailed as an apprenticeship or degree program. Salaries are relatively low.

A Good Fit: For those who do not need a structured educational setting to learn, and who are able to pick up their skills and knowledge on the job.

are aware of any job openings. Maybe your dad's friend works in the construction industry and knows about job openings. Perhaps your high school shop teacher is friends with a flooring contractor who is looking for a helper. A person at a construction association you meet online doesn't know about any current job openings, but can offer you a list of companies that may be hiring in the new year. You get the idea.

■ *Experienced tile installers in the United States can earn more than $71,000 a year.*

You have two types of networks: personal and professional. Your friends and family make up your personal network. Your professional network consists of the following types of people:

- Fellow apprentices and classmates
- Instructors
- Your family or friends who know people in the construction or floor installation industries
- People you meet at construction industry events
- People you meet online, including at social networking sites such as LinkedIn and Facebook (try the Builders Talk Group)

Here are some general rules and tips for networking:

- You can network almost anywhere—you never know who can steer you to a job.
- Be specific when you tell people you're looking for a job. Tell people what type of job you're seeking (in the construction industry, with a government agency, at a private company), where you want to work (close to home, willing to move for the right position), and your educational background. This will save people time.

- Don't be afraid to contact people in the construction industry you don't know—most people are happy to help young people learn more about job opportunities.
- Help your classmates, fellow apprentices, and family and friends who are also looking for jobs.

Check Out Job Boards. Job listings can be found on internet job boards that are hosted by professional associations, government agencies, and businesses. At many of these sites, you can search by geographic region, salary, job type, employer name, and other criteria. While you're not ready to look for a job, it's useful to read some job listings to see what types of skills and educational backgrounds are in demand. Here are a few popular job boards:

- https://www.linkedin.com
- https://www.usajobs.gov (U.S. government job board)
- https://www.jobbank.gc.ca (Canadian government job board)
- https://www.gov.uk/jobsearch (United Kingdom government job board).

Join and Use the Resources of Unions and Professional Associations. Unions are organizations that help workers obtain higher pay and better benefits and working conditions for their members. They also offer apprenticeships, continuing education opportunities, and other resources. Unions are also called *trade unions* and *labor unions*. About 14 percent of all construction workers (including flooring installers) in the United States belong to a union. Some flooring installers are members of the United Brotherhood of Carpenters and Joiners of America and the International Union of Painters and Allied Trades. These unions represent trades workers in both the United States and Canada.

Professional associations are another good source of job leads, as well as continuing education classes, certification programs, career information, publications and blogs, and networking events. Most countries have at least one professional association for flooring installers. Here are some major professional associations for flooring installers around the world:

- American Concrete Institute (United States)
- Australian Timber Flooring Association
- Australian Tile Council

Did You Know?

Flooring installers who are certified typically earn higher salaries and have better job opportunities than those who are not certified. Why? There is a lot of competition in the flooring industry, and companies and consumers only want to hire the most-skilled workers. The certification process typically involves the completion of classes and the passing of an examination. The following organizations have certification programs:

- Ceramic Tile Education Foundation
- International Certified Floorcovering Installers Association
- International Masonry Institute
- International Standards & Training Alliance
- International Union of Bricklayers & Allied Craftworkers
- National Tile Contractors Association
- National Wood Flooring Association
- Tile Contractors' Association of America
- Tile Council of North America

- Carpet Institute of Australia
- International Certified Floorcovering Installers Association (United States and Canada)
- International Standards & Training Alliance (United States and Canada)
- The Masonry Society (international)
- Mason Contractors Association of America (United States)
- National Concrete Masonry Association (United States)
- National Guild of Master Craftsmen (Ireland)
- National Institute of Carpet and Floorlayers (United Kingdom)
- National Terrazzo and Mosaic Association (United States)

Average Salaries for Trades Workers in the United States

Salaries for flooring installers are not as high as those in many other trades careers. Here's how their pay ranks compared to other trades workers.

- Elevator Installers and Repairers: $76,860
- Electricians: $56,650
- Plumbers, Pipefitters, and Steamfitters: $56,030
- Brickmasons and Blockmasons: $53,440
- Sheet Metal Workers: $51,080
- Carpenters: $48,340
- Heating and Cooling Technicians: $48,320
- Tile and Marble Setters: $44,770
- Plasterers and Stucco Masons: $44,070
- Carpet, Floor, and Tile Installers and Finishers: $43,950
- Roofers: $42,080
- Painters and Paperhangers: $41,430

- National Tile Contractors Association (United States)
- National Wood Flooring Association (United States)
- Tile Contractors' Association of America (United States)
- Tile Council of North America, Inc. (United States, Canada, and Mexico)

How Much Can I Earn?

Flooring installers do not make as much money as many other types of trades workers. In fact, carpet, floor, and tile installers and finishers in the U.S. earn average pay ($43,950 according to the U.S. Department of Labor, USDL) that typically falls at the lower end of the pay scale for trades workers. The average salary for all construction workers in the U.S. is $48,900. But it's important to note that pay ranges vary by type of flooring installer. Those with specialized skills, certification, or lots of experience earn more than those who do not have these traits. Here's a sampling of salaries (low, average, and high earnings) for workers in different flooring specialties:

- Carpet installers: $20,810 to $44,310 to $80,440+
- Floor layers (except carpet, wood, and hard tiles): $23,260 to $42,370 to $68,720+
- Terrazzo workers and finishers: $25,980 to $45,990 to $75,470+
- Tile and marble setters: $24,200 to $44,770 to $71,260+

Average Earnings by Employer

Flooring installers who work for certain types of employers earn higher average salaries than those in other sectors. For example, the USDL reports the following average annual earnings for carpet installers by employer:

Salaries for Tile and Marble Setters by U.S. State

Earnings for tile and marble setters vary widely by state based on demand and other factors. Here are the five states where employers pay the highest average salary and the states in which employers pay the lowest salaries.

Highest Average Salaries:
1. New York: $72,080
2. Massachusetts: $65,570
3. Hawaii: $61,120
4. Missouri: $58,250
5. Connecticut: $55,650

Lowest Average Salaries:
1. Oklahoma: $31,250
2. New Mexico: $31,550
3. Florida: $31,870
4. Texas: $32,130
5. Arkansas: $32,240

Source: U.S. Department of Labor

- Building finishing contractors: $46,250
- Home furnishings stores: $40,580
- Foundation, structure, and building exterior contractors: $38,740
- Residential building construction: $36,360

Making the highest salary is not the most important thing in life. Finding a job that makes you happy and that also offers good **fringe benefits** is just as important.

Top Earners

The top 10 percent of flooring installers earn anywhere from $68,000 to $80,000 or more depending on their specialty. You can earn a high salary if you have a lot of experience, oversee other workers, or live in an area where there is a shortage of flooring installers.

Flooring installation company owners can make $75,000 to $150,000 or more, depending on the size of their businesses.

If you work as a salaried employee, you'll receive fringe benefits such as medical insurance, a pension, and other benefits. If you own a contracting business, you'll have to provide your own benefits.

■ *Flooring installation company owners in the United States can make $75,000 to $150,000 or more a year.*

Text-Dependent Questions

1. What high school classes should you take to prepare for a career in floor installation?

2. What is a union?

3. How do salaries for flooring installers compare to those of other types of trades workers?

Research Project

Talk to flooring installers who trained for the field in different ways (apprenticeship, college, assistant to experienced installer). Ask them the following questions: How long did the training last, and what did it involve? What did you like and dislike about this type of training? If given the chance, would you train the same way? What advice would you give to a young person regarding training to enter the field? Prepare a report that summarizes the interviews. Try to determine what would be the best training approach for you.

ON THE JOB
Interview with a Professional

Jason Kolodziej is a project manager at Costello Wholesale Floor Company in Mokena, Illinois.

Q. Can you tell me about your company?

A. We are a flooring wholesaler supplying contractors, designers, and the general public with the finest products in the area. In addition, we strive to maintain our reputation as the leading installation provider in the area. We specialize in new construction and remodeling for any size commercial or residential project.

Q. What inspired you to get into this field?

A. I have a passion for helping people achieve their dreams. Giving people their dream kitchens, bathrooms, and homes is what inspires me.

Q. Can you tell me about a day in your life on the job?

A. Everything starts with the selection process. From there we go over details such as designs and patterns for each individual area using drawings and blueprints. After all material is ordered and received, I schedule an installation date. At that time, I review the project with my team and the project is executed. Each day is different, which is a good thing. Acquiring new business is a big part of my daily work also. Learning about new products and systems is a common thing. You're constantly learning in this job, which is nice because it keeps you on your toes.

Q. What is the most rewarding part of your job?

A. I take pride when people say, "in your professional opinion," when asking about details of their project. I love seeing the transformation of a space. The gratification of seeing the before and after is amazing. Referrals are one of the most rewarding parts of my job. Knowing that my team and I did our job for someone and they're so happy with our work that they refer people to us is the biggest compliment. Seeing people's reactions after projects are complete is also a great feeling. You can see it in their

48

eyes that they're so happy and they say things like, "I love my bathroom because of what you guys did," is really awesome.

Q. What kind of personal traits do you think are important for people in your career?

A. Perception to be able to listen and understand what the customer is looking for. Integrity to perform each project the right way and by using the proper materials (taking NO shortcuts). Patience to help customers throughout the entire process. Honesty to give your customers the correct answers when they ask for your professional advice. Diligence to work hard and get the project done in a timely manner. You have to have passion to be in this line of work. You have to treat every project like it is being done at your own home.

Q. What advice would you give to someone who is considering a career in your field?

A. Make sure they have the traits listed above. Have an open mind to always be learning what is new and staying on top of current trends and designs. Honesty is key; if customers lose confidence in you, the outcome will not be good. Good problem-solving ability is also key. In construction, nothing is perfect so being able to assess and fix problems is a daily task. Make sure that you're a team player. The people you work with are a huge part of your success in this line of work.

Q. What is the employment outlook in the flooring industry?

A. Employment opportunities are on the rise. The beauty of any tradesman is that we cannot be replaced by robots or technology. Not everyone wants to work with their hands, but the people who do will always have a job in the flooring industry. Construction is one of the last things made in America.

Q. How is technology changing the industry?

A. Technology is making the industry more efficient. There is software that is able to do takeoffs from blueprints more efficiently and more accurately than a human can do. Also, the technology in sundries (mortar, grout, etc.) is much more advanced than before. The use of satellites to take pictures of stone quarries makes for more realistic views of tile. Technology will continue to make the industry more efficient with new products and tools.

■ *Flooring installers need good dexterity and hand–eye coordination. Above, an installer uses a portable angle grinder to cut floor tile.*

Words to Understand

ethnic group: A collection of people who have a shared connection based on their homeland, cultural heritage, history, ancestry, language, or other factors.

invoicing: The process of sending a customer a bill for work that has been completed.

rehab: In the construction industry, to restore or rehabilitate a structure, typically a home.

soft skills: Personal skills that people need to develop to interact well with others and be successful on the job. They include communication, work ethic, teamwork, decision making, positivity, time management, flexibility, problem-solving, critical thinking, conflict resolution, and other skills and traits.

CHAPTER 5

Key Skills and Methods of Exploration

What All Flooring Installers Need

A career as a flooring installer is interesting and fun because you get to use both your hands and your head to install and repair carpeting, tiles, wood floors, and other flooring material. This career is physically demanding, but you'll also need strong soft skills. Here are the most-important traits for flooring installers:

- **Good dexterity, hand–eye coordination, and hand speed.** You'll need these skills to deftly place carpeting, tile, wood planks, and other types of flooring so that it looks visually appealing and is properly aligned. You'll need to work quickly (before adhesives harden) and accurately to keep jobs on schedule.

■ *Flooring installers need good communication skills because they often work in teams.*

- **Physical strength and stamina.** Some flooring materials such as stone and wood can be heavy, so you'll need good strength. Additionally, you'll spend much of your day stooping, bending, reaching, and kneeling, which can be tiring and hard on your body. Flooring installers who are in good shape can better handle the physical challenges of the job than those who do not stay physically fit.

- **Good color vision.** Tile installers and marble setters must be able to identify small color variations, as well as choose amongst the most attractive color combinations when installing tile to create the best finished look.

- **Artistic ability.** Terrazzo, tile, and carpet square installers need a good sense of how different colors, textures, and patterns work together to create an attractive finished product.

- **Detail oriented.** Details count in the flooring industry. For example, if you fail to leave expansion space along each wall when you install a wood floor, the floor might expand in humid conditions and buckle. If you make an error measuring the dimensions of a room when installing carpeting, the carpeting will be too long or short. If you own a flooring installation business and fail to keep track of customer appointments and **invoicing**, order supplies, and perform other daily duties, you won't be in business long.

- **Communication and customer-service skills.** Successful flooring contractors must be polite, courteous, friendly, and patient with customers. They need to be able to explain—in everyday language—various flooring options to customers (for example, the differences in quality, durability, and price between wood and laminate flooring, or between carpeting and vinyl flooring).

- **Ability to work independently.** You'll need to be able to follow instructions without supervision, as well as effectively manage your time.

- **Teamwork/interpersonal skills.** Many flooring installers work in small teams. To be a good teammate, you'll need to learn how to work with people from different backgrounds, **ethnic groups**, ages, and experience levels.

- **Business skills.** Contractors not only need good communication and customer-service skills, but they also must have good marketing skills, the ability to use their math skills to create bids for jobs, skill at managing staff, and be comfortable using office management software, the internet, and social media.

- **Honesty and strong ethics.** You should always be honest with your customers—recommending the best flooring materials for their needs—not those that will make you the most money. When you're about to install flooring at a home, you should think about it as your own—and give your customer the best value for their money.

Exploring Flooring Installation as a Student

There are many ways to explore this field and the construction industry in general. Check out the following activities to build your skills and knowledge—and have some fun in the process:

Take Some Classes. You don't have to wait till you start an apprenticeship or enroll in college to begin learning about construction practices and the skills you'll need to run a business. In fact, you can start as early as middle school or high school by taking classes that will teach you about the building trades, the science behind adhesives and floor installation, and the basics of running a business. Begin with shop classes. In these courses, you'll learn how to use hammers, saws, chalk lines, trowels, and other tools. You'll build things. You'll learn how to troubleshoot and solve

■ *Computer science classes will come in handy if you decide to open your own flooring business.*

problems—skills flooring installers use every day. You may even get a chance to install or repair a floor. Finally, you'll learn how to be safe on the job. All kinds of injuries and accidents can happen on the job if you don't follow safety rules.

Math classes are extremely important. Flooring installers use math to calculate the amount of building materials that will be needed to cover a floor, to determine the right combination of ingredients when mixing adhesives, to prepare estimates for customers, and to perform many other tasks.

Business, accounting, finance, and marketing classes will come in handy if you plan to launch your own flooring installation company.

Here are some other classes that will be useful as you prepare for a career as a flooring installer:

- physics
- chemistry
- English/writing
- computer science

■ *A high school construction class builds a tiny house from the ground up:*

Try Out Some Tools. Using different tools provides a great introduction to the construction industry. It's also fun. Who doesn't want to pound a few nails, snap a chalk line, or saw a piece of wood or tile. Be sure to take safety precautions (gloves, goggles, hearing protection, etc.) when experimenting with tools. You can find tools in your shop class, your parents' garage, at a hardware store, or at a local library (some

■ *Trying out tools is a great way to learn more about the construction industry. Above, a teen uses a circular saw in shop class.*

have tool lending programs). If you don't know how to use a certain tool, ask a parent or shop teacher for help. YouTube also has great videos that provide tips on how to use tools.

Build Something! Now that you've tried out a few tools and obtained a little experience in shop class, it's time to build something. Perhaps you could help your mom and dad install new carpeting, tile, or wood flooring in your home. But if that's not possible, you could buy a small number of tiles or a few pieces of carpeting, adhesives, and other supplies and experiment with laying carpet, tiles, or other types of flooring. Ask your parents or shop teacher for guidance during this process. Don't be scared to try something new. Have fun and learn about some of the challenges installers encounter during a project. Who knows. You might learn that your floor installation skills are better than you first thought. Check YouTube for how-to videos. And check out *Black & Decker Wood Floors: Hardwood, Laminate, Bamboo, Wood, Tile, and More* to learn some flooring terms and get some tips on how to get started.

■ *Learn how to lay floor tiles:*

Watch Home-Improvement Shows. There are many shows on television, cable, and the internet that show tradespeople at work and the big picture of a building being rehabbed or built from scratch. These will provide an overview of construction techniques and the types of issues encountered by flooring installers and other trades workers. Here are a few to check out:

- *This Old House:* http://www.pbs.org/show/old-house
- *Holmes on Homes:* http://www.hgtv.com/shows/holmes-on-homes
- Many shows on HGTV: http://www.hgtv.com/shows

Join or Start a Construction Club at Your School. Becoming a member of your school's construction club is an excellent way to learn more about the trades and various construction careers. In such a club, you'll learn about carpentry, masonry, and other construction specialties. You'll learn to use hammers, chisels, saws, grinders, and other tools. You'll view presentations by construction workers (including flooring installers) and tour construction sites. Some clubs even offer their services to their local communities. They help skilled trades workers build new homes, or repair damaged ones, after tornadoes, hurricanes, and floods. Others help the elderly or those who do not have a lot of money to keep their homes in good repair. If your school doesn't have a construction club, start one with your classmates!

Job Shadow or Conduct an Information Interview with an Installer. In a job shadowing experience, you'll observe a flooring installer at work for a few hours or an

Tips on Participating in a Job Shadowing Experience

- Be friendly, be enthusiastic, and listen closely as the flooring installer talks about his or her job and work duties.
- Do not touch any equipment, tools, or building materials unless given permission to do so.
- Wear any safety gear that is required.
- Turn off your cell phone.
- Wear business casual clothing—skip the shorts and t-shirts.
- Prepare a list of questions and be prepared to take notes.
- Be ready to answer questions about your career interests and goals.
- Conduct yourself professionally at all times during the job shadowing experience.
- Say thank you at the end of the job shadowing experience, and send a thank-you email or handwritten note the next day.

entire day. This allows you to see what it's really like to be an installer. You can ask installers questions about their work. You may even get a chance to use a trowel or hammer and install some flooring.

During an information interview, you just talk with a person about his or her career. Interviews can be conducted on the phone or in-person, and typically last from ten to twenty minutes. You could even conduct the interview via email if someone is not available for a phone or in-person meeting. Ask the following questions during the interview:

- Why did you decide to enter this career?
- Can you tell me about a day in your life on the job?
- What's your work environment like?

Sources of Additional Exploration

Contact the following organizations for more information on education and careers in construction and floor installation:

Australian Timber Flooring Association
https://www.atfa.com.au

Australian Tile Council
https://www.australiantilecouncil.com.au

Carpet Institute of Australia
https://www.carpetinstitute.com.au

Ceramic Tile Education Foundation (United States)
https://www.ceramictilefoundation.org

Finishing Trades Institute International
http://www.finishingtradesinstitute.org

International Certified Floorcovering Installers Association (United States and Canada)
https://www.cfiinstallers.com

International Masonry Institute
http://imiweb.org/tmt

International Standards & Training Alliance (United States and Canada)
https://installfloors.org

National Guild of Master Craftsmen (Ireland)
http://www.nationalguild.ie

National Institute of Carpet and Floorlayers (United Kingdom)
http://www.nicfltd.org.uk

National Terrazzo and Mosaic Association (United States)
http://www.ntma.com

National Tile Contractors Association (United States)
http://www.tile-assn.com

National Wood Flooring Association (United States)
https://www.nwfa.org

Tile Contractors' Association of America (United States)
https://www.tcaainc.org

Tile Council of North America, Inc. (United States, Canada, and Mexico)
http://www.tcnatile.com

■ *A high school student learns how to read blueprints during a tour of a construction site.*

- How do you stay safe on the job?
- What are the most important personal and professional qualities for people in your career?
- What do you like best and least about your career?
- What is the future employment outlook for flooring installers? How is the field changing?
- What can I do now to prepare for the field (classes, activities, projects, etc.)?
- What do you think is the best educational path to becoming a flooring installer?

Your school counselor, construction club teacher-mentor, shop teacher, and family or friends can help arrange a job shadowing opportunity or information interview. Professional associations and unions can also help you find candidates.

Read About Flooring Installation. Reading floor installation blogs, articles, and journals is a good way to learn industry lingo, understand common issues faced by installers, and discover trends in the industry. Some of the terms and topics might seem overwhelming at first, but as you read more you'll start to understand the world of installation. Check out Chapter 2: Tools of the Trade and Chapter 3: Terms of the Trade for additional help. Here are some popular publications and resources:

- Flooring America's Flooring and Design Blog: http://www.flooringamerica.com/blog
- Stories in Stone: https://www.ntma.com/stories-in-stone
- *Hardwood Floors:* https://www.nwfa.org/technical-resources.aspx
- Carpet and Flooring Glossary: https://www.homeadvisor.com/r/carpet-and-flooring-glossary

■ *A woman and her daughter use home design software to create their dream kitchen and living room.*

Play Designer and Create a Floor. The National Wood Flooring Association offers a Design a Room tool at its website (https://www.woodfloors.org/design-room.aspx) that allows users to select the type of wood, shade, size, board width, angle of the wood, and other criteria in a variety of room settings. The site will give you a basic idea of the questions both customers and flooring installers must address before the start of a project. Many large carpeting, tile, and wood flooring companies have similar websites. Check out their websites to continue to experiment with flooring designs.

Text-Dependent Questions

1. Why must flooring installers be detail oriented?

2. What are two ways to explore flooring installation as a student?

3. Name three organizations that offer useful resources about education and careers in flooring installation.

Research Project

Participate in an information interview or job shadowing experience with a flooring installer. Write a one-page report that summarizes what you learned. Present it to the members of your shop class or construction club.

■ *Job opportunities for flooring installers are expected to be strong in Canada.*

Words to Understand

Baby Boomer: A person who was born from the early-to-mid 1940s through 1964.

cost-effective: Doing something that is effective based on its cost. For example, walking a mile instead of driving, to save money. An example of an action that is not cost-effective would be paying your employees more than what you are being paid to do a job; you would make no money.

economy: Activities related to production, use, and trade of services and goods in a city, state, region, or country.

recruitment firm: A company that helps job-seekers find jobs, as well as assists employers who are seeking to fill open positions.

CHAPTER 6

The Future of the Flooring Installation Occupation

The Big Picture

High quality, attractive flooring is an extremely important part of any home, business, or other building. The presence of hardwood, marble, or terrazzo floors in a home increases its value. And businesses like to wow customers and clients with stunning hardwood, stone, or other types of floors. And regardless of whether we're trying to sell our homes or impress people, we need floors. As a result, there will always be strong demand for flooring installers.

But despite the strong need for flooring installers and other trades workers, there's a shortage of skilled professionals in some countries. Globally, workers in the skilled trades were cited by employers as the most in-demand career field,

■ *Natural disasters, such as floods, unfortunately create many job opportunities for flooring installers.*

according to the human resource consulting firm ManpowerGroup. By continent or region, skilled trades workers topped the most in-demand list in the Americas, Europe, the Middle East, and Africa. They ranked fourth in the Asia-Pacific region. The

recruitment firm Michael Page recently conducted research to determine demand for specific careers by country. It found that there is a shortage of tiling workers in Canada, Sweden, Russia, and Australia.

■ *Learn about the shortage of construction workers and the benefits of working in the trades versus going to college and having a lot of debt:*

Job opportunities for flooring installers in the United States are also predicted to be good. In fact, employment for installers is expected to grow by 10 percent during the next decade, according to the U.S. Department of Labor. It reports that "although carpet is still the dominant flooring, other products, including hard flooring such as linoleum and vinyl, are growing in popularity." There will be many new jobs for flooring installers because of the following factors:

- Many **Baby Boomer** installers are approaching retirement age, and there are currently not enough trainees to fill replacement needs.

- The U.S. population is growing, which is creating a residential building boom. Flooring installers will be needed to install flooring in new homes, as well as in businesses, factories, and other structures.

- Natural disasters such as tornadoes, hurricanes, earthquakes, floods, and massive wildfires will create demand for flooring installers and other construction workers. For example, wildfires destroyed at least 8,400 homes and buildings in Northern California in the United States in October 2017. Flooring installers and other construction workers were needed to help rebuild these homes.

Women in Flooring Installation

Women make up about 47 percent of the U.S. workforce, but less than 1 percent of flooring installers. Educational programs, construction associations, trade unions, and others are trying to encourage more women to pursue careers in flooring installation. They say this career is a great option because it offers:

- The opportunity to work with your hands and build something
- Good job security; there will always be a need for people to install and repair floors
- An opportunity to start your own business

Here are a few organizations that support women in the construction industry:

- The Canadian Association of Women in Construction (http://www.cawic.ca) offers membership, a mentoring program, networking events, and a job bank at its website.
- The National Association of Home Builders (http://www.nahb.com) offers a Professional Women in Building group. Members receive *Building Women* magazine, networking opportunities, and the chance to apply for scholarships.
- The National Association of Women in Construction (NAWIC, http//www.nawic.org) offers membership, an annual meeting, and scholarships. It also publishes *The NAWIC IMAGE*.

New Technologies

Technology hasn't changed the flooring industry as much as it has some other construction trades, but the field is certainly different than it was twenty years ago. Here are some ways in which educational training and the work of flooring installers have changed as a result of technology:

- Students learn about flooring installation techniques via smart boards, webinars, and computer simulations. Some students are even required to have their own laptops for class.

- Installers use tablet computers and laptops to review blueprints, diagrams, and installation plans, as well as laser levels and moisture meters (instead of traditional levels and visual examination) to do their jobs more quickly and efficiently.

- Flooring contractors use building information modeling software, a computer application that incorporates a 3D model-based process to more efficiently plan, design, and construct buildings and their flooring components.

- Flooring contractors used to use paper files and a scheduling book to keep their offices organized. Now, they use office and customer management software to create estimates and invoices, schedule appointments, track inventories of equipment and supplies, and do other tasks. In the past, flooring contractors advertised their services through newspaper ads and word-of-mouth. Today, they still use these advertising methods, but now also use the internet and social media to market their businesses and communicate with their employees and customers.

■ *Flooring installers use a tablet computer to review flooring plans at a construction site.*

Technology will continue to change the flooring industry in the next decade, and installers will need to keep their skills up to date by taking continuing education classes offered by professional associations, colleges, and private companies; earning certification credentials to show that they are experts in various specialties; and reading industry publications to keep up with changes in the industry.

■ *Learn more about a prototype of a robotic tiling machine for automated floor tiling:*

■ *An industrial robot at work in a factory.*

Did You Know?

In 2016, China was the leader in producing industrial robots. It accounted for 74 percent of all industrial robots that were produced. Here were the top five producers of industrial robots:

1. China: 87,000

2. Republic of Korea: 41,000

3. Japan: 39,000

4. United States: 31,000

5. Germany: 20,000

Source: Statista.com

Challenges to Employment Growth

We'll always need flooring, but there's a chance that future developments may limit job growth for flooring installers. If the **economy** weakens and another recession occurs, the number of homes and other buildings that are under construction will decrease. This will reduce demand for installers. Flooring installers will still be needed to repair existing floors, but some homeowners and business owners may put off repairs until the economy improves.

Could a robot replace a flooring installer? Not yet, but maybe in the future—especially for large installation jobs. Robots are everywhere these days. The number of industrial robots being produced will grow to 521,000 by 2020, according to the International Federation of Robotics, an increase of 71 percent since 2016. Scientists are developing robotic tiling machines that can install flooring, but none are in widespread use. If robots are used to install flooring, there will be fewer jobs for installers. But there will still be a need for installers to program the robots, check the work of robots, and perform tasks that a robot cannot do. Finally, it's more likely that robotic tiling machines would be used for large construction projects (factories, hospitals, sports stadiums, etc.) rather than in homes and other smaller construction projects because it would not be **cost-effective** to work in homes. As a result, flooring

■ *Strong employment opportunities are expected for carpet installers during the next decade.*

installers will still be needed to work in homes and do other smaller flooring jobs, as well as repair flooring.

Employment opportunities may also decline if many more people enter this field after learning about job shortages. Once the word of worker shortages spreads, more people will enter apprenticeship or other training programs, and the number of jobs will evaporate. In this instance, installers who have specialized knowledge (green construction, new types of flooring, etc.) and who are certified will have the best job prospects. If the number of jobs declines, installers must be ready to move to other states, or even other countries, to find work.

In Closing

Do you like working with your hands to install beautiful flooring? Do you like to solve problems as you build things? Would you like to earn good pay without a four-year degree? If you answered "yes" to all these questions, then a rewarding career as an installer could be in your future. I hope that you'll use this book as a starting point to discover even more about a career as a flooring installer. Talk to installers about their careers and shadow them on the job, use the resources of professional organizations and unions, and try installing a few pieces of old carpeting or cover a small area with tiles to build your skills. Good luck exploring a career in flooring installation!

Did You Know?

- About 125,900 flooring installers are employed in the United States. Tile and marble setters make up 46 percent of this group; carpet installers, 32 percent; floor layers, except carpet, wood, and hard tiles, 13 percent; floor sanders and finishers, 6 percent; and terrazzo workers and finishers, 3 percent.

- Approximately 36 percent of flooring installers are self-employed.

- About 9 percent of workers in the construction industry are women.

Source: U.S. Department of Labor

Text-Dependent Questions

1. Can you name three reasons why employment prospects are good for installers?

2. How do installers use technology to do their jobs better?

3. What are some developments that might slow employment for installers?

Research Project

Try to learn more about robotic tiling machines. What tasks will they be able to perform, and which will still require humans? How will the introduction of robots change the work of floor installers? Write a one-page report that summarizes your findings and present it in science class.

apprentice: A trainee who is enrolled in a program that prepares them to work as a skilled trades worker. Apprentices must complete 2,000 hours of on-the-job training and 144 hours of related classroom instruction during a four- to five-year course of study. They are paid a salary that increases as they obtain experience.

apprenticeship: A formal training program that often consists of 2,000 hours of on-the-job training and 144 hours of related classroom instruction per year for four to five years.

bid: A formal offer created by a contractor or trades worker that details the work that will be done, the amount the company or individual will charge, and the time frame in which the work will be completed.

blueprints: A reproduction of a technical plan for the construction of a home or other structure. Blueprints are created by licensed architects.

building codes: A series of rules established by local, state, regional, and national governments that ensure safe construction. The National Electrical Code, which was developed by the National Fire Protection Association, is an example of a building code in the United States.

building information modeling software: A computer application that uses a 3D model-based process that helps construction, architecture, and engineering professionals to more efficiently plan, design, build, and manage buildings and infrastructure.

building materials: Any naturally-occurring (clay, rocks, sand, wood, etc.) or human-made substances (steel, cement, etc.) that are used to construct buildings and other structures.

building permit: Written permission from a government entity that allows trades workers to construct, alter, or otherwise work at a construction site.

community college: A private or public two-year college that awards certificates and associate degrees.

general contractor: A licensed individual or company that accepts primary responsibility for work done at a construction site or in another setting.

green construction: The planning, design, construction, and operation of structures in an environmentally responsible manner. Green construction stresses energy and water efficiency, the use of eco-friendly construction materials (when possible), indoor environmental quality, and the structure's overall effects on its site or the larger community. Also known as **green building**.

inspection: The process of reviewing/examining ongoing or recently completed construction work to ensure that it has been completed per the applicable building codes. Construction and building inspectors are employed by government agencies and private companies that provide inspection services to potential purchasers of new construction or remodeled buildings.

job foreman: A journeyman (male or female) who manages a group of other journeymen and apprentices on a project.

journeyman: A trades worker who has completed an apprenticeship training. If licensed, he or she can work without direct supervision, but, for large projects, must work under permits issued to a master electrician.

Leadership in Energy and Environmental Design (LEED) certification: A third-party verification that remodeled or newly constructed buildings have met the highest criteria for water efficiency, energy efficiency, the use of eco-friendly materials and building practices, indoor environmental quality, and other criteria. LEED certification is the most popular green building rating system in the world.

master trades worker: A trades professional who has a minimum level of experience (usually at least three to four years as a licensed professional) and who has passed an examination. Master trades workers manage journeymen, trades workers, and apprentices.

prefabricated: The manufacture or fabrication of certain components of a structure (walls, electrical components, etc.) away from the construction site. Prefabricated products are brought to the construction site and joined with existing structures or components.

schematic diagram: An illustration of the components of a system that uses abstract, graphic symbols instead of realistic pictures or illustrations.

self-employment: Working for oneself as a small business owner, rather than for a corporation or other employer. Self-employed people are responsible for generating their own income, and they must provide their own fringe benefits (such as health insurance).

smart home technology: A system of interconnected devices that perform certain actions to save energy, time, and money.

technical college: A public or private college that offers two- or four-year programs in practical subjects, such as the trades, information technology, applied sciences, agriculture, and engineering.

union: An organization that seeks to gain better wages, benefits, and working conditions for its members. Also called a **labor union** or **trade union**.

zoning permit: A document issued by a government body that stipulates that the project in question meets existing zoning rules for a geographic area.

zoning rules: Restrictions established by government bodies as to what type of structure can be built in a certain area. For example, many cities have zoning rules that restrict the construction of factories in residential areas.

Index

Photo Credits

Further Reading & Internet Resources

Addis, Bill. *Building: 3,000 Years of Design*, Engineering, and Construction. New York: Phaidon Press, 2015.

Dykstra, Alison. *Green Construction: An Introduction to a Changing Industry*. San Francisco: Kirshner Books, 2016.

Editors of Cool Springs Press. *Black & Decker Wood Floors: Hardwood, Laminate, Bamboo, Wood, Tile, and More*. Minneapolis, Minn.: Cool Springs Press, 2017.

Editors of Family Handyman. *100 Things Every Homeowner Must Know: How to Save Money, Solve Problems, and Improve Your Home*. New York: Reader's Digest, 2015.

Truini, Joseph. *Installing Floors*. Newtown, Ct.: Taunton Press, 2014.

Internet Resources

http://www.hgtv.com/design/decorating/design-101/flooring-buyers-guide: Visit this website to learn more about the various types of flooring.

http://www.careersinconstruction.ca/en/careers/career-finder: This website from BuildForce Canada provides information on job duties, training, and salaries for floor covering installers, tilesetters, and more than fifty other construction and trades careers.

https://www.bls.gov/ooh/construction-and-extraction/tile-and-marble-setters.htm: This article from the *Occupational Outlook Handbook* provides information on job duties, educational requirements, salaries, and the employment outlook for flooring installers and tile and marble setters.

https://nationalcareersservice.direct.gov.uk/job-profiles/home: This resource from the United Kingdom's National Careers Service provides information on job duties, educational requirements, key skills, salaries, and the work environment for carpet fitters, floor layers, tilers, and others trades professionals.

http://www.byf.org: This web initiative of the National Center for Construction Education and Research offers overviews of more than thirty careers in the trades, videos of trades workers on the job, and much more.

About the Author

Andrew Morkes has been a writer and editor for more than 25 years. He is the author of more than 20 books about college-planning and careers, including many titles in this series, the *Vault Career Guide to Social Media*, and *They Teach That in College!?: A Resource Guide to More Than 100 Interesting College Majors*, which was selected as one of the best books of the year by the library journal *Voice of Youth Advocates*. He is also the author and publisher of "The Morkes Report: College and Career Planning Trends" blog.

Video Credits

Chapter 1: Learn about the work of carpet installers: http://x-qr.net/1Gpn

Watch a beautiful terrazzo floor being installed: http://x-qr.net/1FLn

Chapter 4: Learn some networking do's and don'ts: http://x-qr.net/1Dxf

Chapter 5: A high school construction class builds a tiny house from the ground up: http://x-qr.net/1HeG

Learn how to lay floor tiles: http://x-qr.net/1DYz

Chapter 6: Learn about the shortage of construction workers and the benefits of working in the trades versus going to college and having a lot of debt: http://x-qr.net/1Due

Learn more about a prototype of a robotic tiling machine for automated floor tiling: http://x-qr.net/1DVF